The BOY
Who CONQUERED
EVEREST

Balboa Press books may be ordered through booksellers or by contacting:

Balboa Press
A Division of Hay House
1663 Liberty Drive
Bloomington, IN 47403
www.balboapresspress.com
1-(877) 407-4847

Printed in Canada.

ISBN: 978-1-4019-3117-9

Balboa Press rev. 6/29/2010

www.balboapress.com

Jordan Romero was a regular 9 year old boy. He loved BMX biking, listening to music, hanging out with his friends and family, participating in school activities and studying nature and reptiles. So why would he want to climb the world's tallest mountains? What made him decide to try something so dangerous and difficult?

It all started when Jordan spotted a map of the famous *Seven Summits*, the tallest mountains on Earth's seven continents, including massive Mt. Everest, the tallest of all. Jordan could not take his eyes off of that map; his head was filled with thoughts of snow-covered peaks, jagged rocks, billowing white clouds and deep blue skies.

Four years later, Jordan stood and gazed down at those peaks and cloudy skies from the 29,035 ft. summit of Mt. Everest. He had reached his goal: To conquer the mightiest of mountains and inspire other kids to dream BIG. How did he do it?

This is his story...

"It is not the mountain we conquer, but ourselves."

--Sir Edmund Hillary
The first known person to reach
the summit of Mt. Everest, 1953

The Goal

Jordan

Mt. Everest

The little mural that
inspired a BIG DREAM!

You wanna' do WHAT??

While Jordan's friends and family supported the idea,

others weren't so sure. Jordan explains:

"Some people couldn't understand why I'd want to do something so difficult. But I already loved mountain climbing, and I wanted to set a really big goal for myself--something that my dad and I could do together."

Actually, it wasn't quite that simple.

Before he could tackle the mighty Everest, Jordan would need to prepare himself by climbing many of the world's tallest peaks. This required him to:

1) Obtain permission from each country. (Jordan's dad Paul and stepmother Karen worked REALLY hard to persuade some governments to allow him to go because Jordan was so young.)

2) Gather the right equipment, supplies, and other gear needed for each type of terrain and seasonal climate.

(Jordan would be climbing in deep snow, over icy glaciers, and up sheer cliffs of rock!)

3) Train, train, train some more, and then

Keep
On
TRAINING.

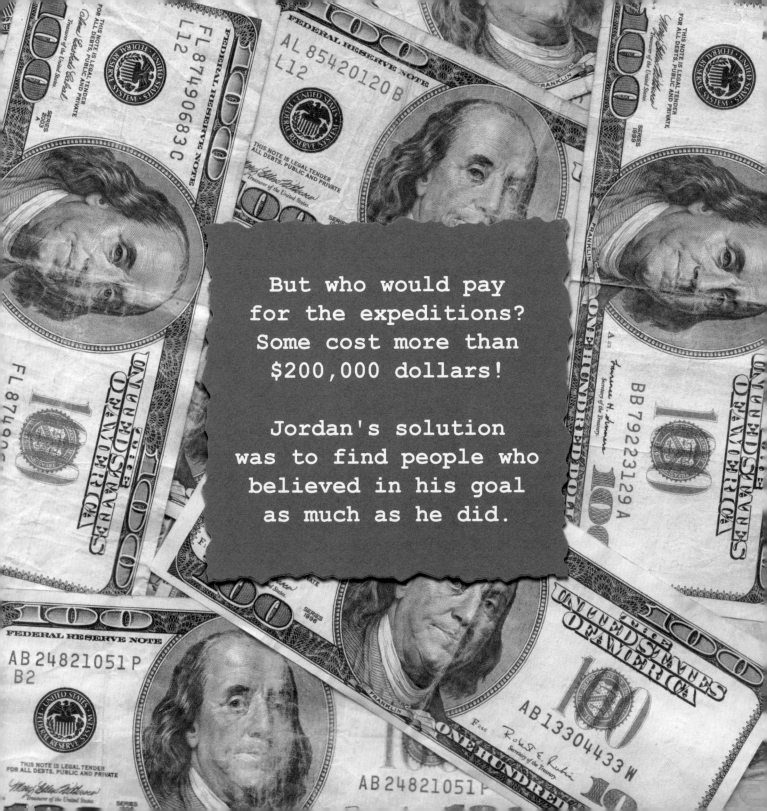

But who would pay for the expeditions? Some cost more than $200,000 dollars!

Jordan's solution was to find people who believed in his goal as much as he did.

"There's no way I could've done these climbs without the support of sponsors and my community.

I spoke to executives from the outdoor industry, and to kids at local schools.

We sold t-shirts and Buffs (fabric bands that you can wear different ways), gained corporate and individual sponsorships, and held some cool fund raising events."

JordanRomero.com

There was no time to waste. Jordan's quest would take hours of work and years to complete.

Paul and Karen got busy planning the upcoming expeditions. There were phone calls to make, meetings to hold, and checklists to write.

Meanwhile, Jordan began a program of tough physical and mental workouts.

This training would prepare him for the extreme conditions and long journey ahead.

Obtain Visas for T...
Check passports
Call expedition companies
Get vaccinations
Call U.S. E...
Co...
G...
Car...
Visit...
Arrang...
Search...
Order foo...
Begin exti...

...port crew
...Russia
...search potential sponsorships
...nize itinerary
...ase additional maps
...existing equipment
...Embassy in Argentina
...ice drills
...Jordan's teacher (arrange homework)
...bassy in Indonesia
...tritional supplements

Order new g...
Thank new sp...
Jordan—scho...

Luckily, Jordan lived in a mountain environment: Big Bear Lake, California (Elevation: 6,750 feet).

Snowshoeing in the San Bernardino Mountains.

In order to prepare himself for the demands of higher-altitude climbing, he ran long distances, trekked on snowshoes, and even climbed California's tallest mountain, Mt. Whitney (14,494 ft), in the middle of winter.

Running on the shores of Big Bear Lake.

Starting up Mt. Whitney ...at 2:30 AM!

"For strength training, I pulled a tire up and down my dirt road.

I carried a 30lb pack on my back and tied a rope and a car tire to my harness and hiked up and down the road about 10 times a day (about 30 minutes).

It turned out to be a great workout for when we had to tow sleds with a lot of gear in them."

Not tire-d yet!

Still not tire-d.

e Team Arrives in Alaska

vel from Big Bear to LAX to Anchorage was

r good buddi _____
d accomodat _____
w us off. The _____
cks and sle _____

ne 11th, 20 _____

ordan
Magazi

is first m _____

's the 3 d _____
ere in _____
rinting _____

www.a _____

lop on there, and _____
...]

June 10th, 2008 | Category: Media, Seven Sum

Jordan Addresses his Eleme
farewell.

The principal of Jordan's school, Kevin Ar
present to his whole school. At the end of
motivating speaker present to the school.
In his sports coat and on the stage, Jord
presentations and brough the roof down.

Jordan Dedicates Climb to Late
Romero

On the approach to high camp 17,000 Jordan st
and told me (dad) that if he succeeds on this clir
climb to his late Uncle Tony Romero.

Two days later from the summit, he tells us on ca
this climb-the highest peak in North America- to r

June 22nd, 2008 | Category: Denali, Seven Summits |

Jordan Summits Denali 20,320´

It's in the books.

Jor ___ as just returned
fl ___

Ma ___ unication. We
co ___

Jord ___ he mountain
dete ___

Denal ___

We will ___

June 21 ___ ummits | 1

Today

I just sent a post from my phone, so pardon if it co
all the kinks. We will send posts from mobile phone
patient, we WILL do our best. Dark/gloomy again h
now start the drive from Anchorage to Tall

Note 1:
A blog was started on Jordan's web site so that his friends, his mom Leigh Anne, and other family members could all follow him on his many adventures.

Jordan's corporate sponsors posted links on the site. Friends and fans used the web site to make donations, directly supporting Team Jordan.

Note 2:
The web site and blog would also be the perfect way to share Karen's photos and videos of Jordan's climbs.

Jordan adopted the motto Ad Alta, Latin words meaning To the Summit.

Ad Alta!

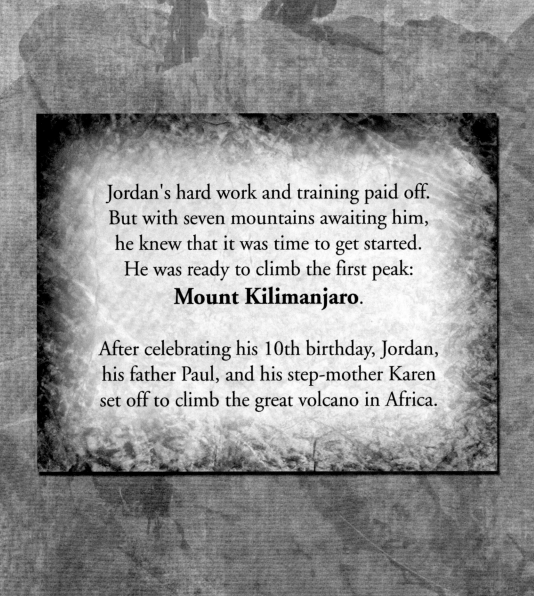

Jordan's hard work and training paid off.
But with seven mountains awaiting him,
he knew that it was time to get started.
He was ready to climb the first peak:
Mount Kilimanjaro.

After celebrating his 10th birthday, Jordan,
his father Paul, and his step-mother Karen
set off to climb the great volcano in Africa.

KILIMANJARO

Summit #1
Mt. Kilimanjaro (aka Kibo)
Continent: Africa
Country: Tanzania
Elevation: 19,340 ft. (5,892 m.)
Reached Summit: July 23, 2006

"We chose the Umbwe climbing route, which is the hardest and also the steepest route to the top.

I started out fast and strong, but my guide, Samuel Kusamba, and the porters kept saying "Polé Polé" (which means "Slowly, Slowly" in Swahili).

Soon they realized that I was doing fine at that speed, so we just kept moving along."

Jordan made new friends on his way up the mountain. He and Samuel became best buddies, and the team of porters (climbing assistants) felt like family.

Jordan passed many groups of fellow climbers heading up or down, and to each of them he proudly greeted "Jumbo!", the Swahili word for "Hello!"

The trail led them from a tropical rainforest into a dry rocky desert. From there they hiked up through thick clouds, shivering in the drippy fog.

Approaching the higher peaks, they trekked carefully through large areas of ice and snow. The air became thinner and thinner. Jordan slowed his pace to avoid high-altitude sickness.

"After three awesome days, we reached the summit of Kilimanjaro (Uhuru Peak). The view was amazing, and I felt proud to have made it all the way up there."

CONGRATULATIONS
YOU ARE NOW AT

UHURU PEAK, TANZANIA, 5895M. AMSL.
running inn

AFRICA'S HIGHEST POINT
WORLD'S HIGHEST FREE-ST
ONE OF W   'S LARG
WELCO

"Then it was time to go DOWN. We began our descent, covering 10,000 feet in 16 hours--nonstop. We spent one last night in a lower camp, then reached the trail head. We finished our trip to Africa by going on a wild safari!"

Jordan's success on Mt. Kilimanjaro
gave him the confidence he needed to continue
his quest. Next on his list was Australia's
Mount Kosciuszko.

At 7,310 feet, it isn't a very tall mountain.
Nonetheless, Kosciuszko is the highest point
on the Australian continent, which qualifies
it as one of the world's *Seven Summits*.

The little mountain offered a few
challenges of its own, but Jordan was able
to reach the summit in less than a day.

Kosciuszko

Summit #2
Mt. Kosciuszko
Continent: Australia
Country: Australia
Elevation: 7,310 Feet
Reached Summit: April 6, 2007

"I thought that this hike would be really easy. I was wrong! It was cold, wet, and super windy."

"The wind slowed us down a bit, but we just kept moving and finally got to the foggy summit."

The cloud-covered summit resembled the surface of a distant planet, with boulders tossed about.

Jordan explored its rocky surface, but the chill winds made for a short stay.

"The hike down seemed to take forever, though I did find a cool worm on the way.

It was nice to get to the car and put on dry clothes. We headed to the nearby city to have some hot pasta and soup. Life is great!"

Mt Kosciuszko (2,228 metres)

Below is the text of the sign which was placed here in 1940 to celebrate the centenary of the first recorded ascent of Mt Kosciuszko.

From the valley of the Murray River the Polish explorer Paul Edmund Strzelecki ascended these Australian Alps on 15th February 1840.

A 'pinnacle, rocky and naked, predominant over several others' was chosen by Strzelecki for a point of trigonometrical survey. 'The particular configuration of this eminence', he recorded, 'struck me so forcibly by the similarity it bears to a tumulus elevated in Krakow over the tomb of the patriot Kosciuszko, that, although in a foreign country, on foreign ground, but amongst a free people, who appreciate freedom and its votaries, I could not refrain from giving it the name of Mount Kosciuszko.'

This commemorative plaque was originally unveiled by the Consul General of the Republic of Poland for Australia, New Zealand and Western Samoa, Ladislas Adam de Noskowski Esq. on the 17th February 1940.

Early visitors

It is highly unlikely that Strzelecki was the first person to climb Mt Kosciuszko.

The Aboriginal people of the Monaro and groups from the southern tablelands, south coast and northern Victoria visited these higher peaks for thousands of years to feast on the bogong moths which gather here in summer and to conduct trade and perform cultural and spiritual ceremonies.

Stockmen began visiting the mountains from the 1830s in search of summer pasture and it is probable that some of them would have climbed the mountain.

Change of name

In 1997 the Geographical Names Board of NSW agreed to a proposal that the spelling be changed to 'Kosciuszko', the correct spelling of the name of the famous Polish freedom fighter.

The board accepted that Strzelecki spelt the name with a 'z'.

With two of the Seven Summits under his belt, Jordan spent the next several months preparing for climb #3: Europe's **Mount Elbrus**.

This mountain would test Jordan's climbing skills on snow and ice, and would represent his greatest technical challenge so far.

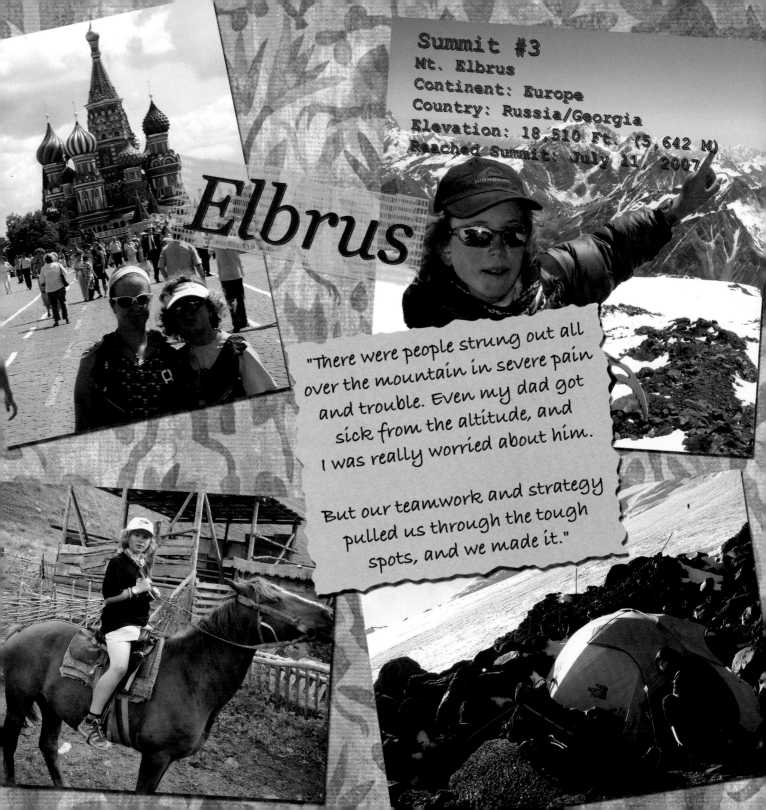

Elbrus

Summit #3
Mt. Elbrus
Continent: Europe
Country: Russia/Georgia
Elevation: 18,510 Ft. (5,642 M)
Reached Summit: July 11, 2007

"There were people strung out all over the mountain in severe pain and trouble. Even my dad got sick from the altitude, and I was really worried about him.

But our teamwork and strategy pulled us through the tough spots, and we made it."

Jordan acted as team leader, helping his ill father and keeping the group focused. This made his parents very proud.

Jordan's team camped for 13 hours to get their bodies conditioned to the altitude. At the summit they were greeted by brutal, gusting winds.

"Bagging this summit was the BEST early birthday present. I turned 11 the next day, and we headed for home. It was time for a little break."

"But I wouldn't rest for long, because I'd be spending the next 5 months training for my biggest challenge yet: Mount Aconcagua--Yikes!"

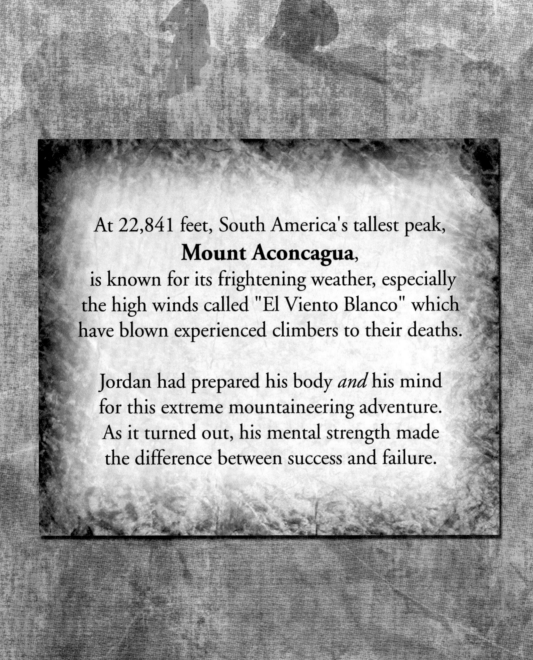

At 22,841 feet, South America's tallest peak,
Mount Aconcagua,
is known for its frightening weather, especially
the high winds called "El Viento Blanco" which
have blown experienced climbers to their deaths.

Jordan had prepared his body *and* his mind
for this extreme mountaineering adventure.
As it turned out, his mental strength made
the difference between success and failure.

SUMMIT #4

Mt. Aconcagua
Continent: South America
Country: Argentina
Elevation: 22,841 Ft. (6,962 M)
Reached Summit: December 30, 2007

"I was THIS close to wanting to turn around and go back.

My body was screaming 'Turn around', but my mind said 'No!'"

No one under 14 is allowed to climb Mt. Aconcagua. To get an exception permit, 11 year-old Jordan had to prove his health and abilities to a doubtful panel of doctors and a judge.

At last he received his permit, but he was monitored closely.

Fewer than 20% make it to the top of Aconcagua. Even Jordan started with a nine person team. But as the going got tougher, his team members dropped out. Jordan, Paul and Karen were the only three who kept pushing themselves all the way to the summit.

The tallest mountain in North America is
Mount McKinley.
The native Inuit people of the region call it
Denali. Both names are officially recognized.

A climb in the summer season would give Jordan
his best chances for good weather. Even so, it was
going to be extremely cold and the conditions
could be unpredictable. It was possible to be stuck
in a tent for days at a time waiting for a blizzard
to stop and the icy winds to settle down.

Jordan's endurance would be put to the test.

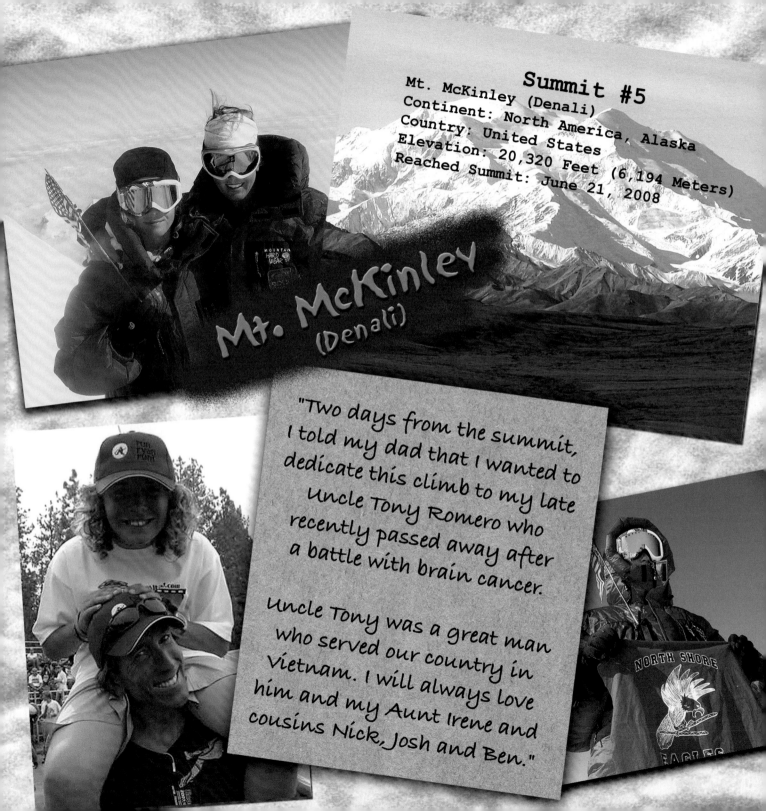

Summit #5
Mt. McKinley (Denali)
Continent: North America, Alaska
Country: United States
Elevation: 20,320 Feet (6,194 Meters)
Reached Summit: June 21, 2008

Mt. McKinley
(Denali)

"Two days from the summit, I told my dad that I wanted to dedicate this climb to my late Uncle Tony Romero who recently passed away after a battle with brain cancer.

Uncle Tony was a great man who served our country in Vietnam. I will always love him and my Aunt Irene and cousins Nick, Josh and Ben."

Jordan had to be very careful. Some of the slopes plunged down into deep, narrow crevasses with no chance of escape. Every move was thought out --like a deadly game of chess.

Sometimes Jordan got exhausted from the physical effort in the thin, high-altitude air. Then he'd think of the support of his family and friends, remembering that he was also climbing for THEM.

"The best part of the climb was the summit ridge -- the last 100 yards before the summit. It was the coolest and also the scariest. One side plummeted down 3,000 feet and the other was a 1,000 to 2,000 foot drop."

"The ridge was a thin blade of wind-blown snow. We were roped in and we had to clip onto fixed anchor posts. It was a beautiful day. The sky was bright blue, and it's an experience I will never forget for the rest of my life."

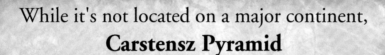

While it's not located on a major continent,
Carstensz Pyramid
is recognized in the climbing world as one of the
Seven Summits because Mt. Kosciuszko is on the
Australian continental shelf, a separate landmass.

Jordan decided to include Carstensz to eliminate
any doubts about his official climbing record.
Carstensz (also called *Puncak Jaya*) juts high above
a lush rain forest in the area of Irian Jaya, claimed
by Indonesia and Papua New Guinea.
Its steep, jagged terrain gave Jordan plenty of
opportunities for rock climbing using ropes.

Summit #6
Carstensz Pyramid (aka Puncak Jaya)
Continent: Australia, Oceania
Country: Papua New Guinea/Indonesia
Elevation: 16,024 ft. (4,884 m.)
Reached Summit: September 2, 2009

Carstensz Pyramid

"Our helicopter flew into a canyon with giant rock walls and waterfalls spewing toward us--like being in a video game. There was nothing but steep jungle all around us. An emergency landing right then would have been impossible.

We searched for the Base Camp, which was hidden in fog. Suddenly, we were surrounded by clouds; everything was white. One of the pilots looked back at us and signaled (the "cut" across the neck).

So, back down to the airport we went, feeling relieved and disappointed at the same time. But mostly RELIEVED."

Jordan fell in love with the people of Indonesia and Papua. Their warm smiles and kindness made a huge impression on him.

For Carstensz, he had to pack a lot of equipment. He'd be using advanced rock climbing techniques on the mountain's rough limestone surface.

The challenges were many as Jordan scaled the sheer rock walls. He made his first "Tyrolean Traverse" in which he was suspended from a rope while slowly pulling himself across a 40 foot ravine.

As he reached the summit, Jordan was grateful for the long hours of rope training he'd practiced at home.

"I dedicated this climb to the Bhandari family of Big Bear, who lost their 5 year-old son Kushan in a hit-and-run accident. I was climbing for Kushan, and thinking about my family and friends. This made it easier for me to focus."

"Looking back on these past 6 climbs I feel that I grew, not only in my physical skills, but also mentally. This would serve me well as I faced the toughest expedition of my life: Mount Everest."

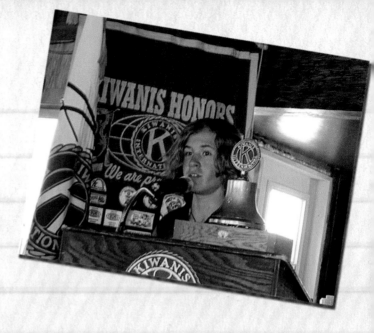

Back home in California, Jordan spoke
to schools and service clubs, telling them
about his adventures and future goals.

"I got this idea that maybe I could use my outdoor experiences to inspire people--especially kids-- to get outside and be healthy.

I could share my goal-setting formula: how I take a big goal, break it into small pieces, then celebrate each smaller victory.

Climbing Mount Everest was a goal that would show kids that it's OK to dream BIG."

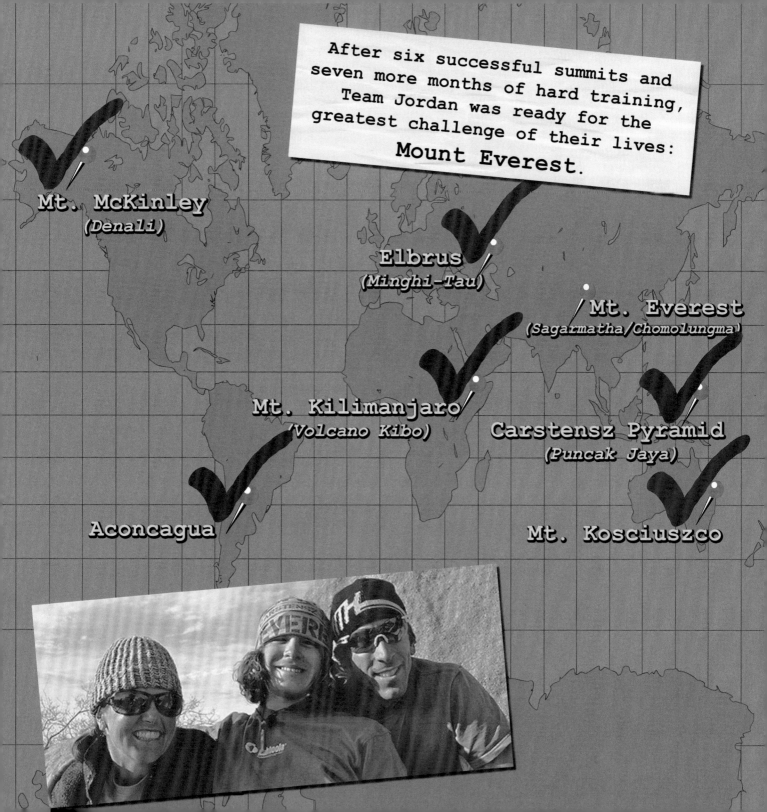

After six successful summits and seven more months of hard training, Team Jordan was ready for the greatest challenge of their lives: **Mount Everest.**

Mt. McKinley
(Denali)

Elbrus
(Minghi-Tau)

Mt. Everest
(Sagarmatha/Chomolungma)

Mt. Kilimanjaro
(Volcano Kibo)

Carstensz Pyramid
(Puncak Jaya)

Aconcagua

Mt. Kosciuszco

The Conquest

Mount Everest.
The very name of this mighty mountain captures
the imagination of people around the world.
The tallest mountain on earth, Everest is known
for its icy, rocky terrain and unpredictable weather.
Winds roar across its surface at 100 mph (62 kph),
the air temperature can reach -40° F (-40° C),
and shifting glaciers create rock slides and icefalls.

Jordan knew the dangers, but he was well-prepared
and ready to attempt his greatest goal yet:
To stand at the top of the world.

SUMMIT #7
Mt. Everest (Chomolungma/Sagarmatha)
Continent: Asia
Countries: China(Tibet)/Nepal
Elevation: 29,035 Ft. (8,850 M)
Reached Summit: May 22, 2010

"I really have dreamed about standing on top of the world since I was a little kid.

I don't feel like I'm rushing; Everest just happens to come right now when I'm 13, and I don't think that my age matters so much."

"OK, we packed a LOT of stuff: 13 bags of gear, medical supplies, food, supplements, cameras, plus an amazing satellite phone!"

"I got to borrow the actual down-filled suit worn by Johnny Strange, who'd completed all Seven Summits by the age of 17."

"At L.A. International Airport, we managed to get our pile of bags checked in, and eventually boarded a long flight to Hong Kong."

In Kathmandu, Jordan was welcomed like a star! But there was a lot of preparation to do, and not a moment to waste.

Karen went right to work setting up the team's communication equipment, while Paul met with the three Sherpas (guides) who would accompany them up Mount Everest.

Jordan was fitted with an oxygen mask that would be his lifeline in the higher altitude zones of Everest.

The Sherpas gave him instructions regarding rapid weather changes and hazards on the mountain.

Then there were visas and permits to pick up, gear to inspect and test, and food to organize and pack.

"The Friendship Bridge crosses from Nepal into Tibet (China). At the border station we passed through Chinese customs, then loaded our gear into a truck for a ride to the town of Nyalam."

"We spent the night in Nyalam, elevation: 12,300 feet (3,750 m)! This was the first stop on a 5 day drive to the Everest Base Camp. These rest stops helped our bodies slowly adjust to higher and higher altitudes."

Team Jordan's next stop was the small village of Tingri, elevation 14,268 ft (4,348 m). They explored the area, and Jordan caught his first glimpse of Mt. Everest in the distance.

Meanwhile, Karen continued to update Jordan's web site and other social media sites.

"After a 5 hour drive on a bumpy dirt road, we made it to Base Camp on the north side of Everest. The elevation is around 17,000 feet (5,100 m), the air is thin and dry, and there are no trees --just millions of broken rocks."

"Our camp cook, Kumar, made us a great lunch with burgers and fries! Then two Tibetan Lamas (priests) did a Puja ceremony with offerings to the mountain, asking for permission to climb. Tibetans call the mountain Goddess Mother of the Earth."

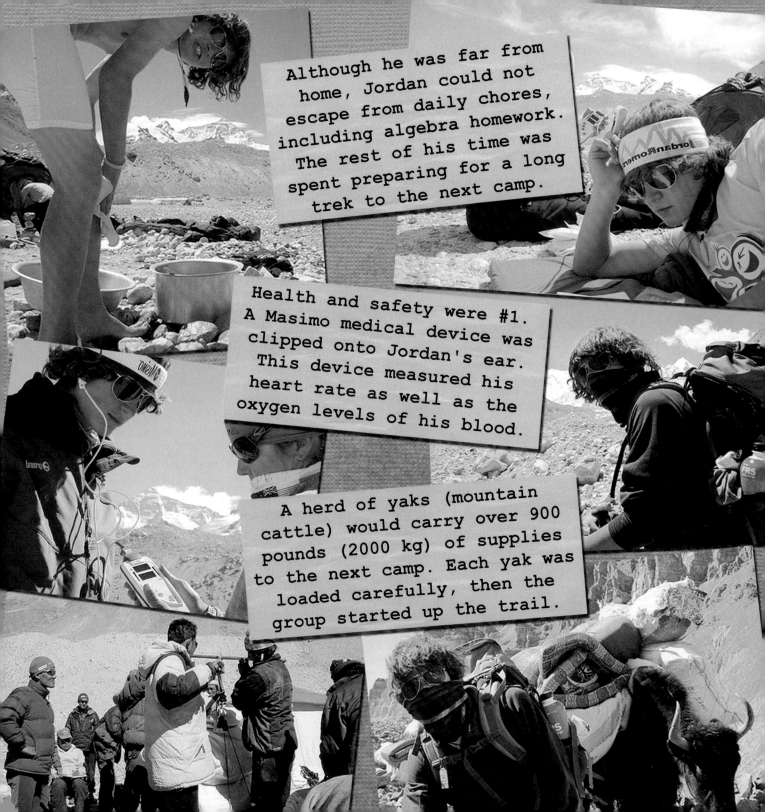

Although he was far from home, Jordan could not escape from daily chores, including algebra homework. The rest of his time was spent preparing for a long trek to the next camp.

Health and safety were #1. A Masimo medical device was clipped onto Jordan's ear. This device measured his heart rate as well as the oxygen levels of his blood.

A herd of yaks (mountain cattle) would carry over 900 pounds (2000 kg) of supplies to the next camp. Each yak was loaded carefully, then the group started up the trail.

"We trekked with our yaks up to the Advanced Base Camp (ABC). It was rough, but I could see the summit the whole time! At ABC we celebrated with new friends from the Chinese Team. Awesome people."

"After resting at ABC, we started our first REAL climbing up to the North Col (a Col is a saddle-shaped ridge). Most of the climb was on slick ice, so we wore crampons (spikes) on our boots."

Summit
29,035 ft/8,850 m

2nd Step
28,140 ft/8,577 m

1st Step
27,890 ft/8,500 m

Camp 3
27,390 ft/8,300 m

Camp 2
24,750 ft/7,500 m

Camp 1
23,000 ft/7,000 m

Advanced Base Camp
21,300 ft/6492 m

In the weeks to follow, Team Jordan would climb up and down and up again between the camps on Mount Everest.

This was exhausting work, but necessary to prepare their bodies for the high altitude and carrying gear to stock the higher camps.

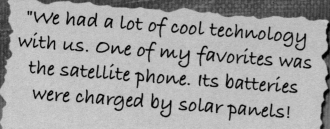

"We had a lot of cool technology with us. One of my favorites was the satellite phone. Its batteries were charged by solar panels!

I called my mom and my sister Makaela almost every day, which made me feel less homesick."

Led by Ang Pasang Sherpa, the team began their steep climb to the higher camps.

Slowly, carefully, they proceeded up the ropes, stopping to catch their breath every so often.

They spent a night at Camp 1 to adjust to the altitude of 23,000 feet (7,000 m).

The following day they returned to ABC and enjoyed a hot meal from Kumar the cook.

MAY

Jordan waited at Base Camp for clear weather up on the mountain. He spent most of his time resting, exercising, eating, and doing homework.

He met climbers from all over the world, and even received a special blessing from Monk Tashi at the Rongbuk monastery.

				5	6	7	8
9	10	11	12	13	14	15
16	17	18	19	20	21	22

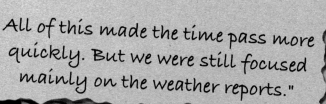

"Even though it was a long wait at Base Camp, I actually had a blast! It was like our own little village. The Russian team had a huge tent with a flat screen TV, a DVD player and a ping-pong table. We played lots of games, went to parties, and watched movies at night.

All of this made the time pass more quickly. But we were still focused mainly on the weather reports."

Jordan posted a message on his blog thanking everyone who had supported him in any way -- big or small.

He was ready to take on the highest peaks of this great mountain that had been his home for more than a month.

Team Prepares »

« At ABC

Here we go

If you have ever sponsored me, ever bought one of my t-shirts, ever attented one of my taco night fundraisers, or just patted me on the back and wished me good luck...I send to you the most sincere thank you.

Today I leave base camp of Everest and every step I take is finally toward the biggest goal of my life, to stand on top of the world.

Every single one of you have made this possible.

I feel in some way I have succeeded in just getting this far, but on the other hand I am drawn to do something great. Know that it comes from <u>my</u> heart. I hope to make you all proud.

- JordanRomero
"It is not the mountain we conquer, but ourselves." Edmond Hillary

SHARE

May 13th, 2010 | Category: <u>Email Posts</u>

On May 15th, Jordan announced his bid for a summit attempt. His hometown of Big Bear celebrated the exciting news.

After a quick call to Mom, the team packed up and climbed to Advanced Base Camp to plan their big move toward the summit.

Jordan practiced his ice skills, climbing up to 23,000 feet then back to ABC. Along the way, he picked up litter on the trail.

The team moved quickly from Camp 1 to Camp 2, a day ahead of schedule.

They left Camp 2 at 5:30 p.m. the next evening, stopping at Camp 3 only to get fresh oxygen bottles and melt snow to refill their drinking bottles. Then they hiked straight on through the night, heading for the summit.

The summit ridge was the most difficult climbing. The team was relieved to see the sun come up just in time for their final push to the summit.

They reached the summit of Mount Everest at 9:45 a.m. on May 22, 2010.

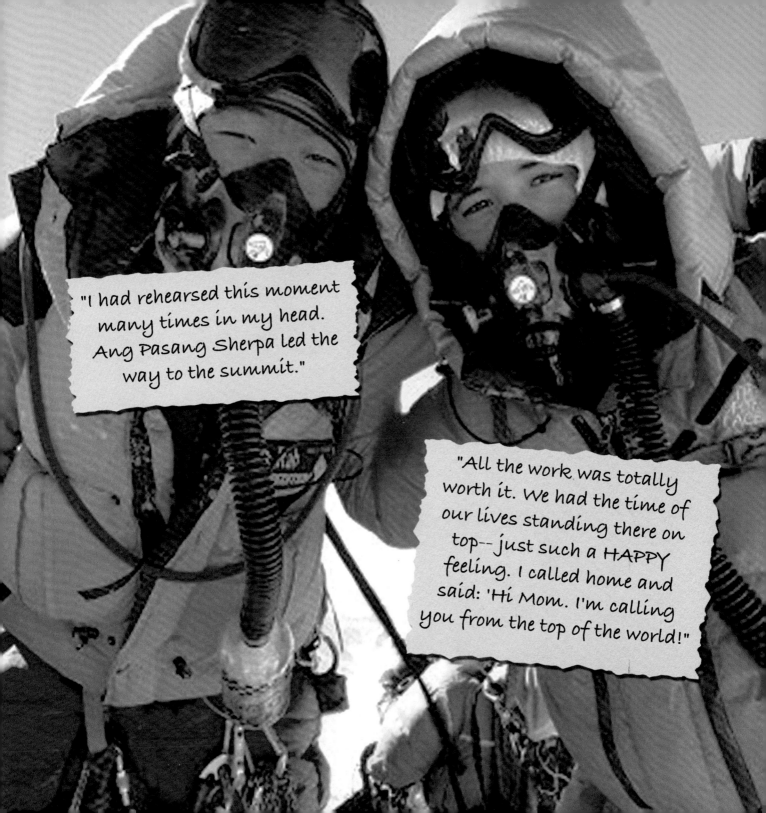

"Find your own Everest."

--Jordan Romero

Team Jordan with their Summit Certificates

What's YOUR Everest?

By reaching the highest summit on Earth, Jordan proved to us all that you CAN have big goals no matter what your age.

He set an example for kids around the world, showing them that they can achieve their own goals and dreams: One step at a time.

Conquer Your Own Everest.
Here are 7 Steps for setting any BIG goal:

7) Ask:"How can this goal help myself *and others?*"

6) Create a plan of action. (you've got to have a plan!)

5) List the skills you will need in order to reach your chosen goal.

4) Identify people and groups who can help you make your goal a reality.

3) List all obstacles to reaching the goal.

2) Set a deadline (date) for completing your goal.

1) Identify your goal, then write it down in detail.

"These are the qualities of a GREAT goal:

Gratitude- Show it, and people will help you.

Respect- Show it, do it, and you will gain it.

Expectations- Set the plan; see it every day.

Action- What's the first step towards reaching your goal? Find it; Make progress every day.

Transformation- Reaching your goal should change you (and the world) for the better."

Anything worth doing -- is worth doing WELL!

If you can dream it, you can achieve it.

Be willing to make mistakes and learn from them.

Give someone a hand and you'll both climb higher.

Never stop believing in yourself.

Be a friend to make a friend.

The best preparation for Tomorrow is to do your best TODAY.

Nobody climbs a mountain alone.
Team Jordan thanks the following supporters:

IN-KIND SPONSORS:
BUFF * Inmarsat * Network Innovations * nuun
* OMEGA XL * POLARTEC * Smith Optics * SOLE *
Team Duke (John Wayne Cancer Foundation)
* Glycemic Research Institute *

PARTNERS:
Adventure Medical Kits * Camelbak * Dr. Calvin
Pramann * Edelrid * Elemental Herbs * Energizer
Batteries * ESRI * FIVE TEN * FRS * HighGear *
Hilleberg The Tentmaker * Jet Boil * Kahtoola *
Kayland * LEKI * Lowepro * Mary Kay * Mountain
Fitness Center * Nepal Trans Himalayan Explorer *
Off Roving * Outdoor Research (OR) * Packit Gourmet
* Petzl * Raw Revolution * Salt Stick * Sherpa
Adventure Travels * Sky High Training * Synergy
Worldwide * Trackme360.com * Vasque

PHOTOS COURTESY OF:
Karen Lundgren * Paul Romero * The Big Bear Grizzly
* Catherine Sandstrom for BigBearNews.com *
* Leigh Anne Drake * Noel Blanc

To learn more about Jordan go to:
www.JordanRomero.com